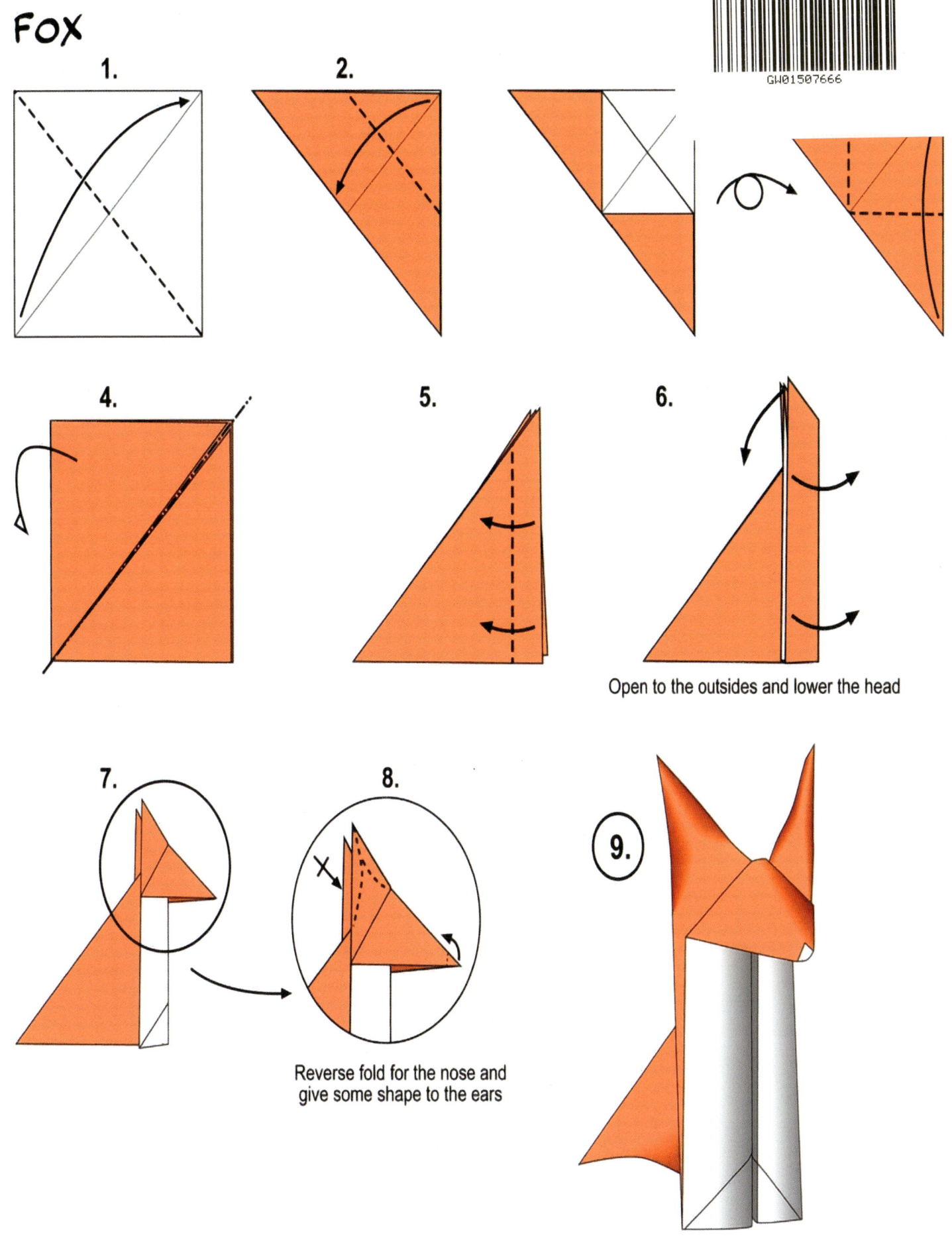

CICADA

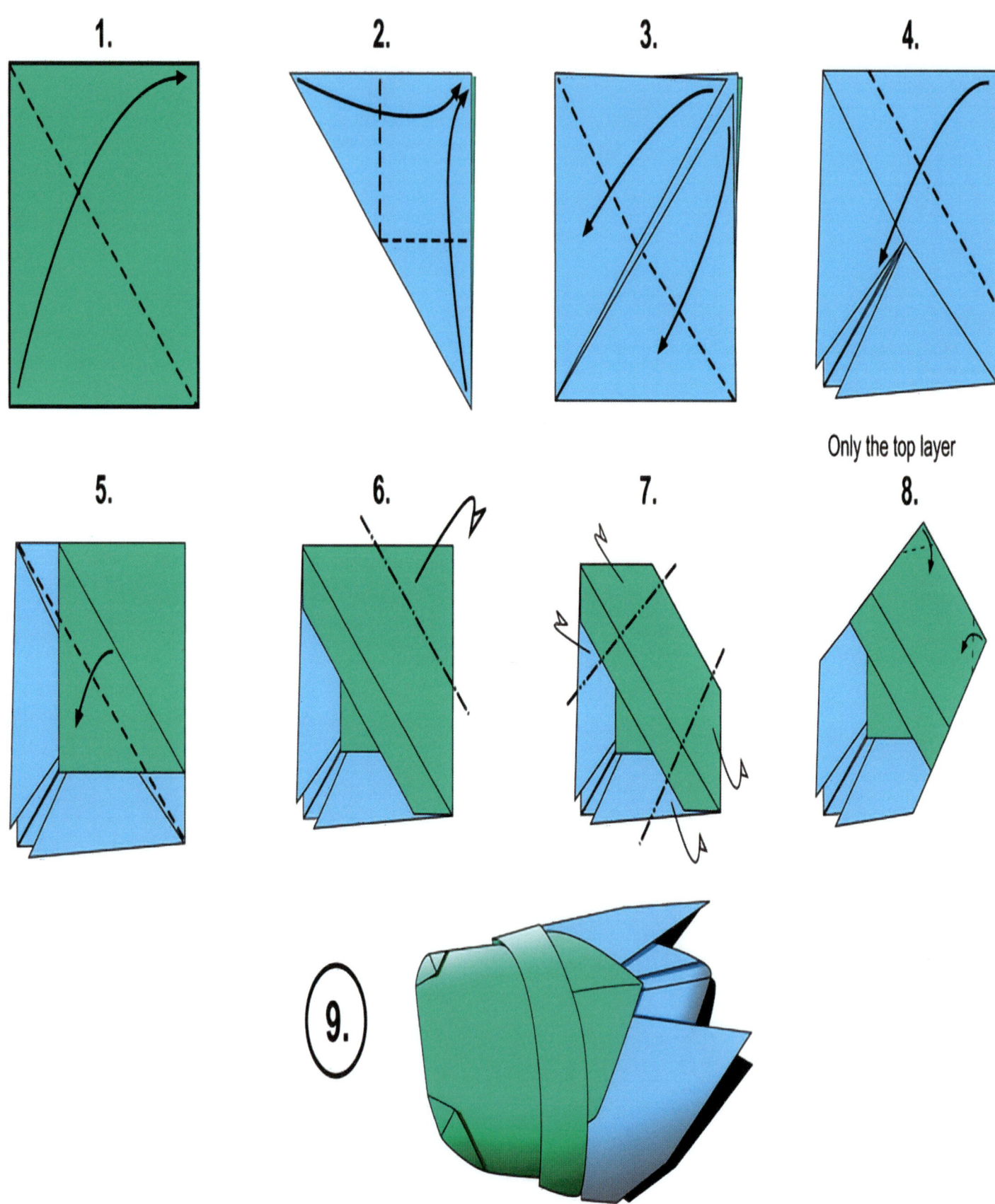

Only the top layer

SANTA

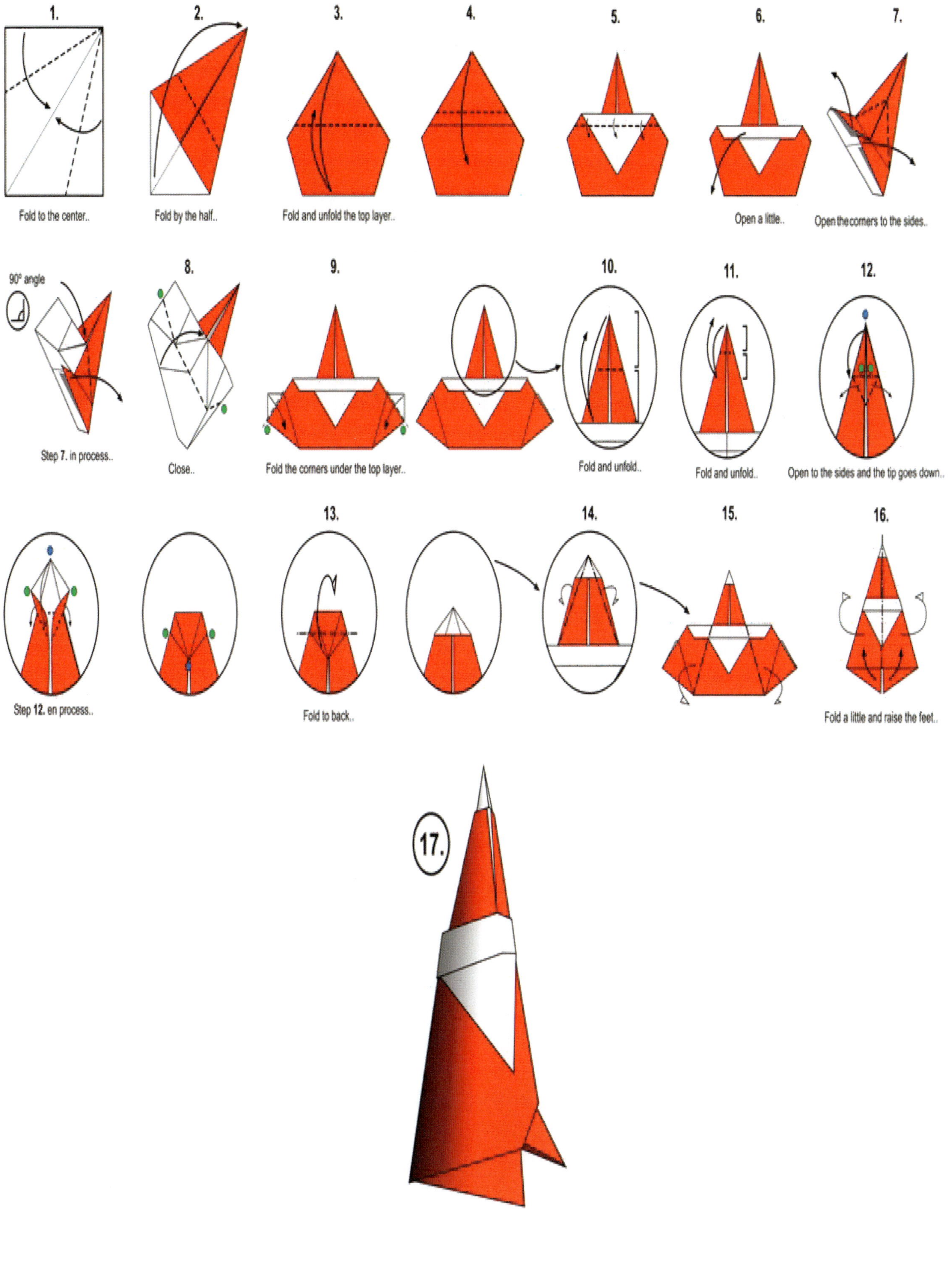

1. Fold to the center..
2. Fold by the half..
3. Fold and unfold the top layer..
4.
5.
6. Open a little..
7. Open the corners to the sides..
8. Step 7. in process.. (90° angle)
9. Close..
10. Fold the corners under the top layer..
11. Fold and unfold..
12. Fold and unfold..
13. Open to the sides and the tip goes down..
14. Step 12. en process..
15. Fold to back..
16.
17.

Fold a little and raise the feet..

17.

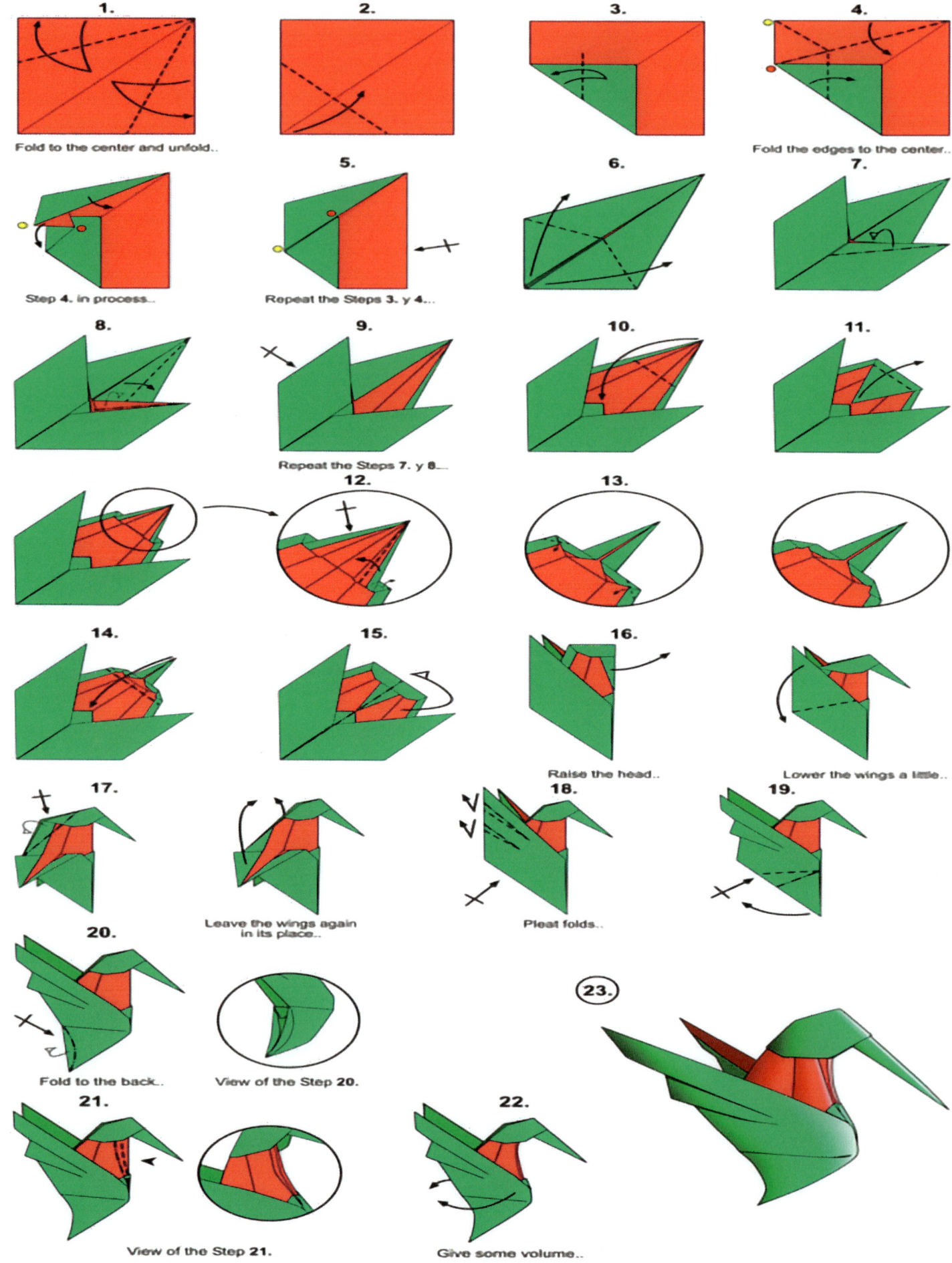

HORSE

1.
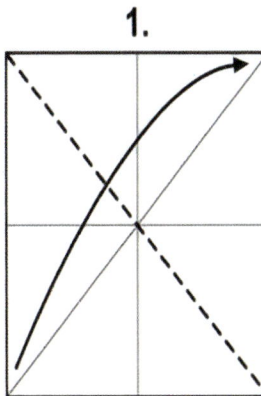

2.
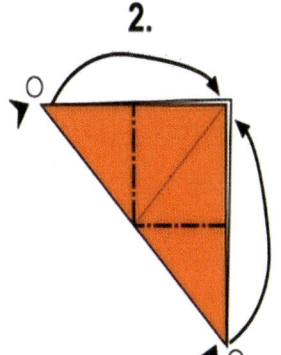
The corners to the inside..

3.
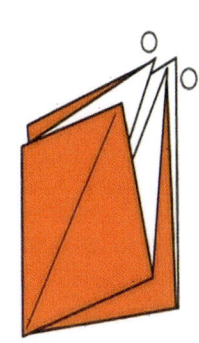
Step 2. in process..

4.
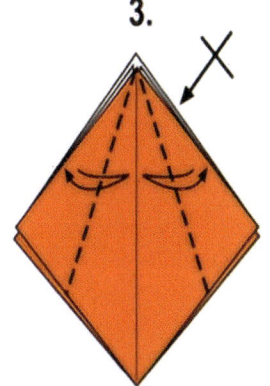
Make the marks in the two sides, front and back..

5.
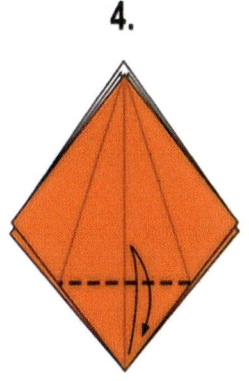

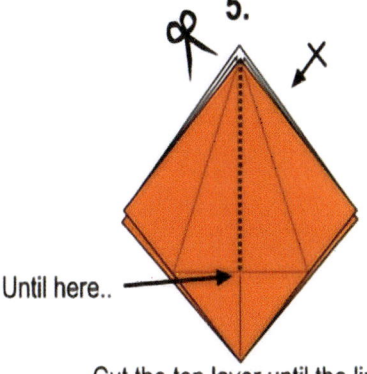
Until here..
Cut the top layer until the line of the previous step..

6.
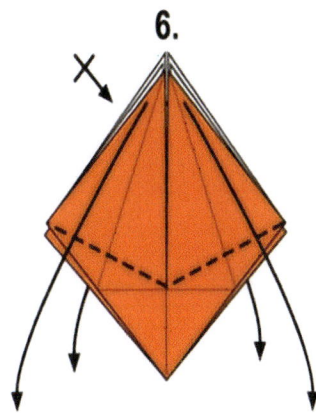

7.
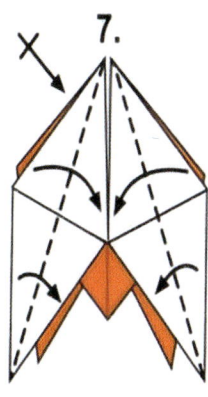

8.
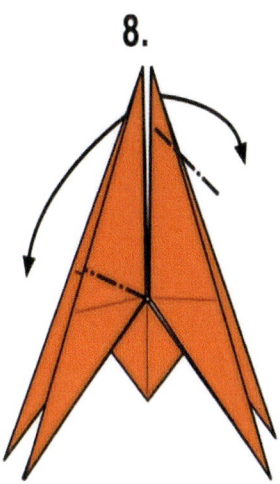

9.
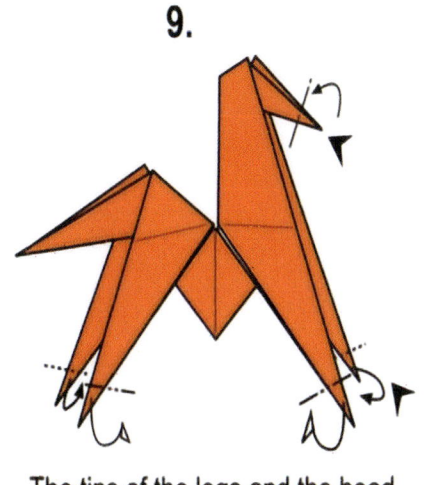
The tips of the legs and the head to the inside..

(10.)
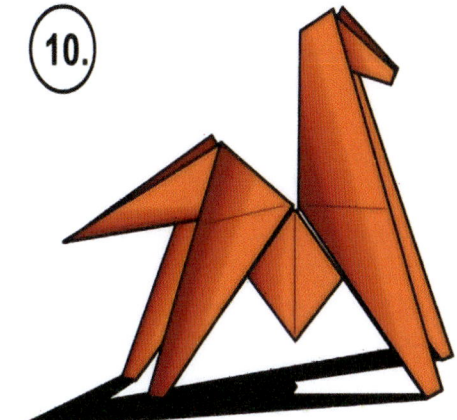

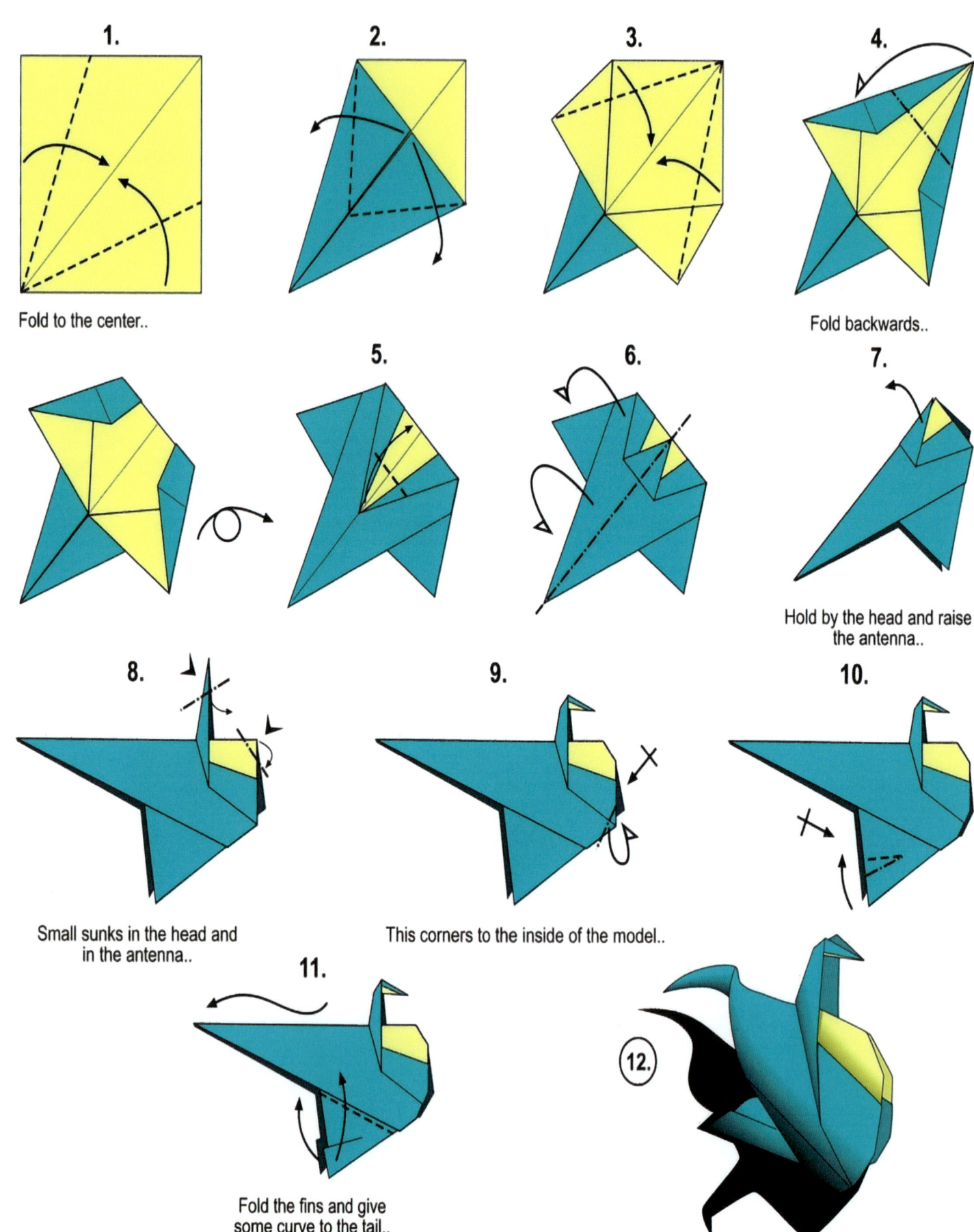

PAJARITA

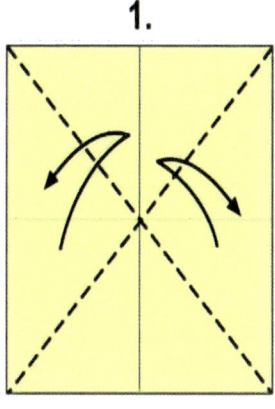

1. Fold and unfold..

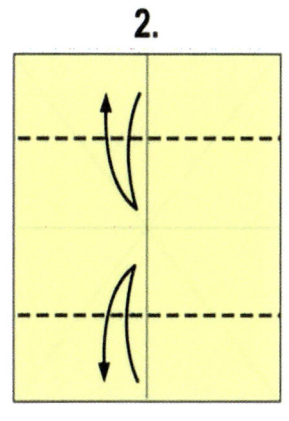

2. Fold and unfold..

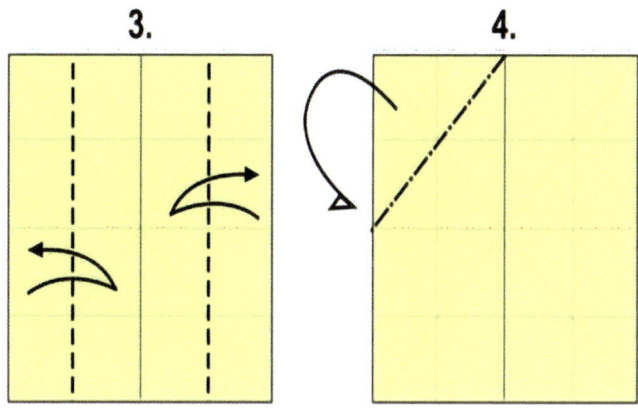

3.

4. The corner to the back..

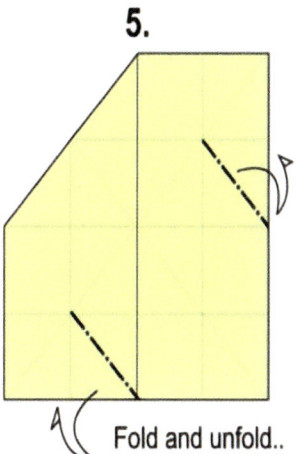

5. Fold and unfold..

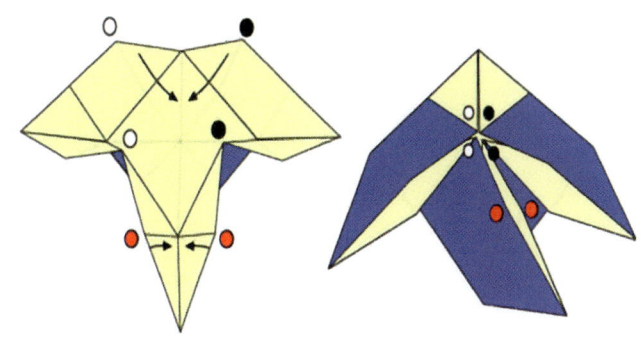

6. The sides to the center..

Step 6. in process - Frontal View -

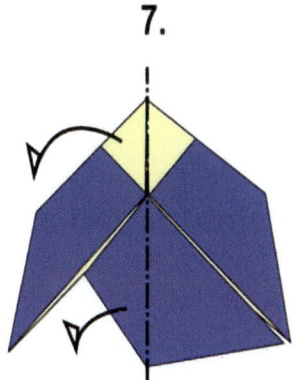

7. Fold by the half..

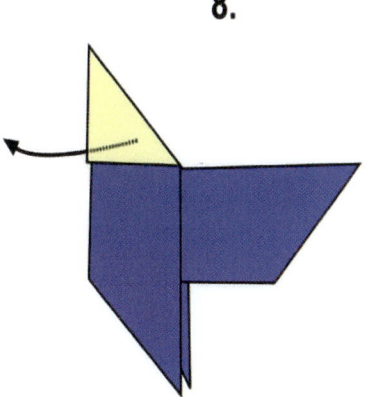

8. Take out the hidden tip..

9.

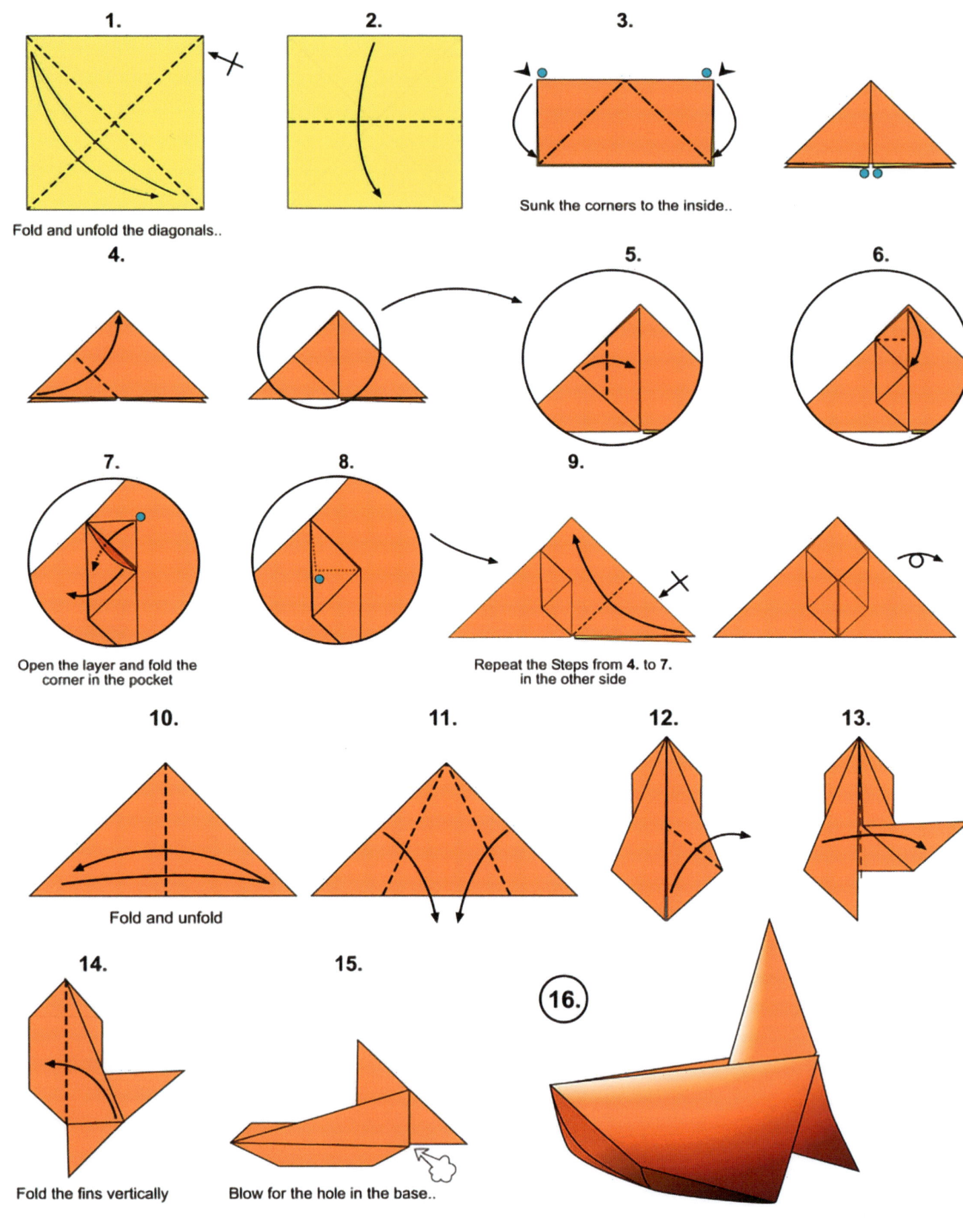

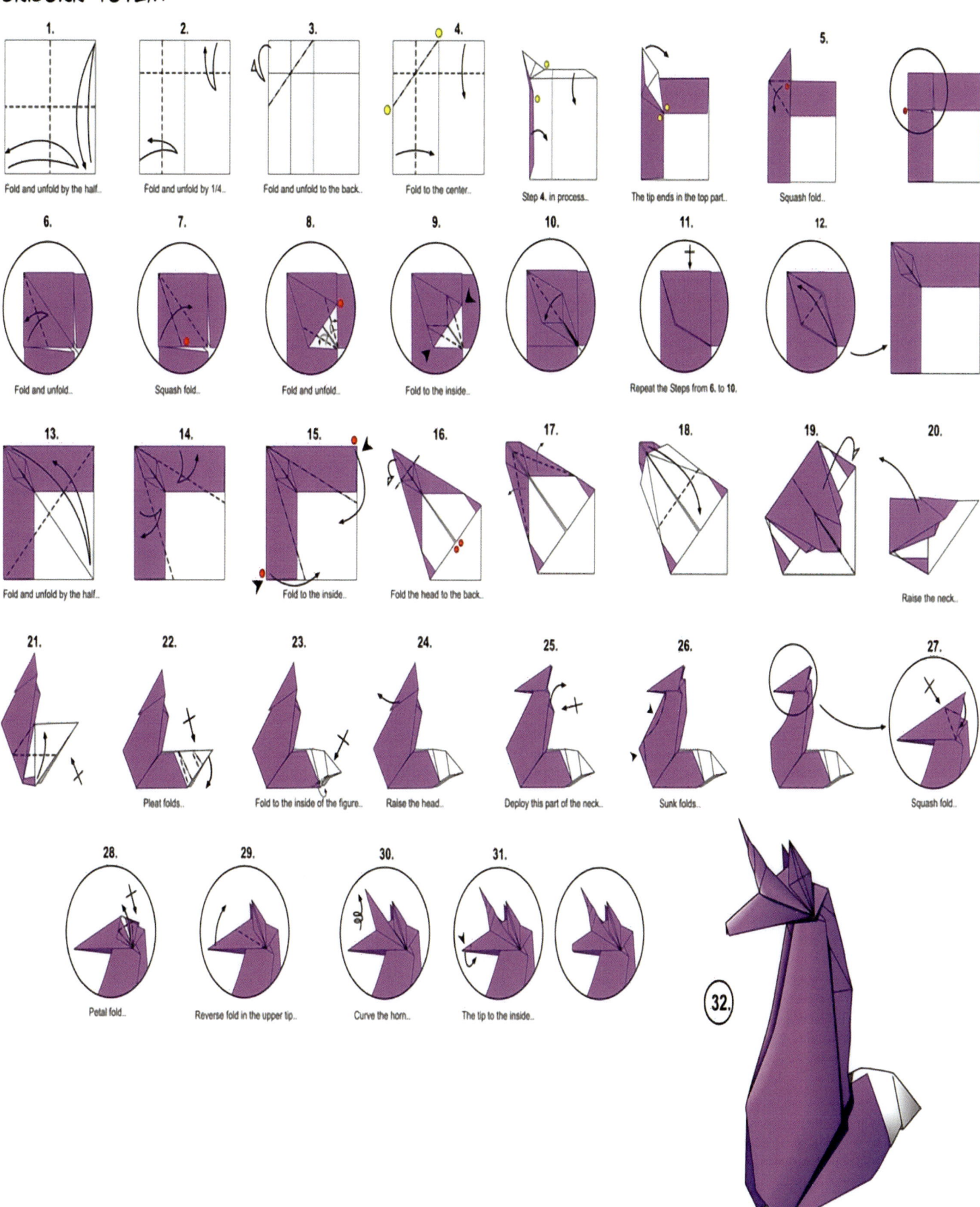

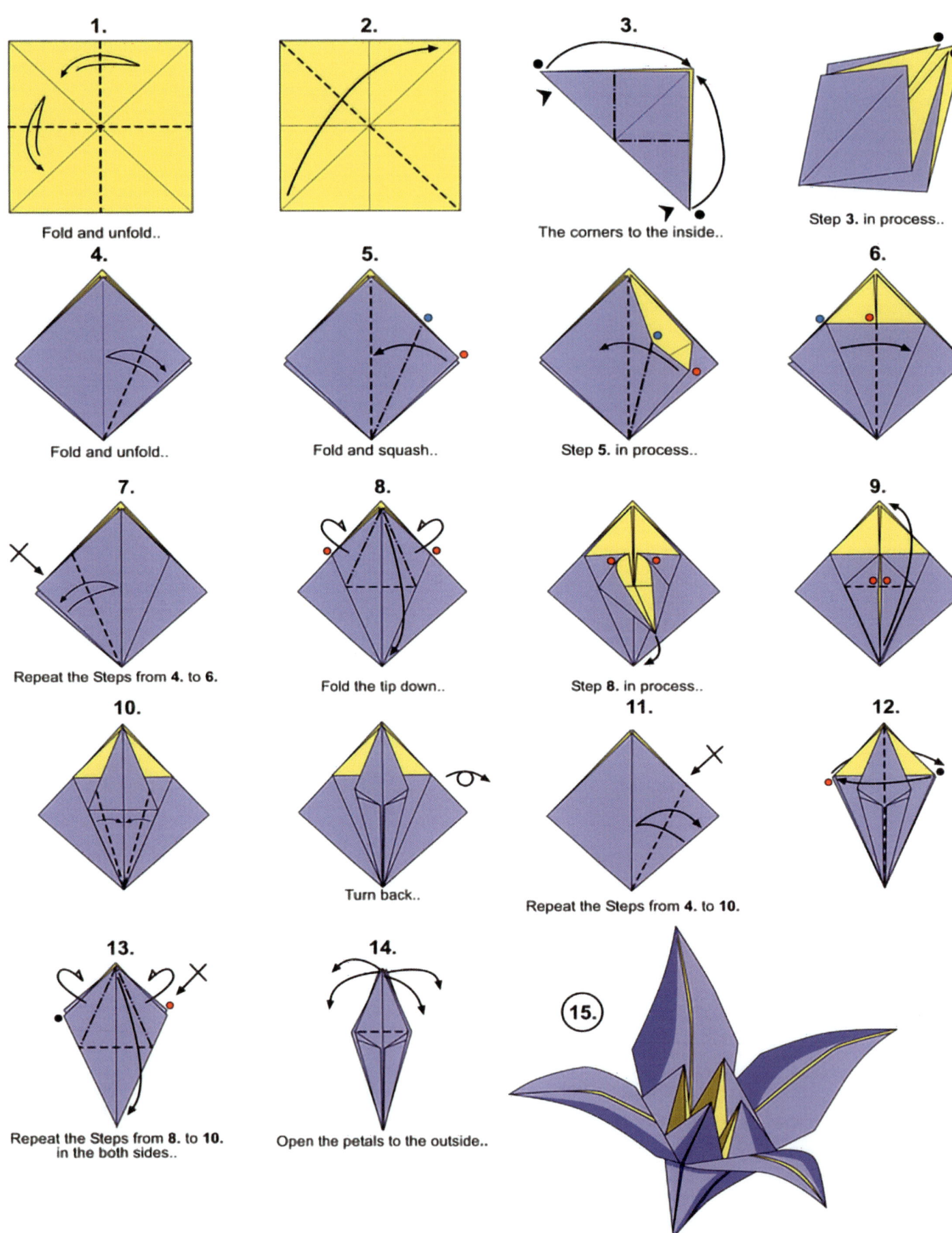

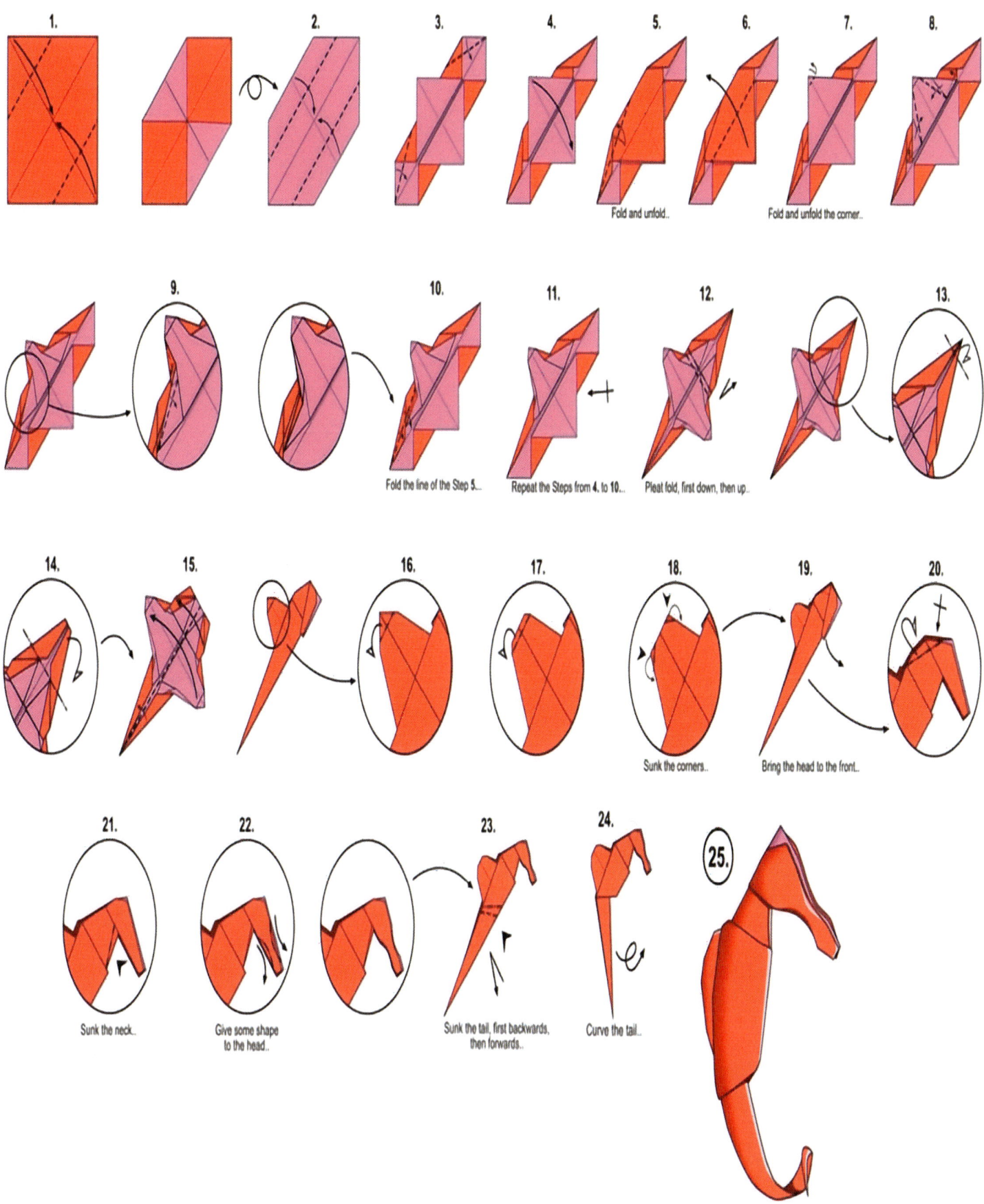

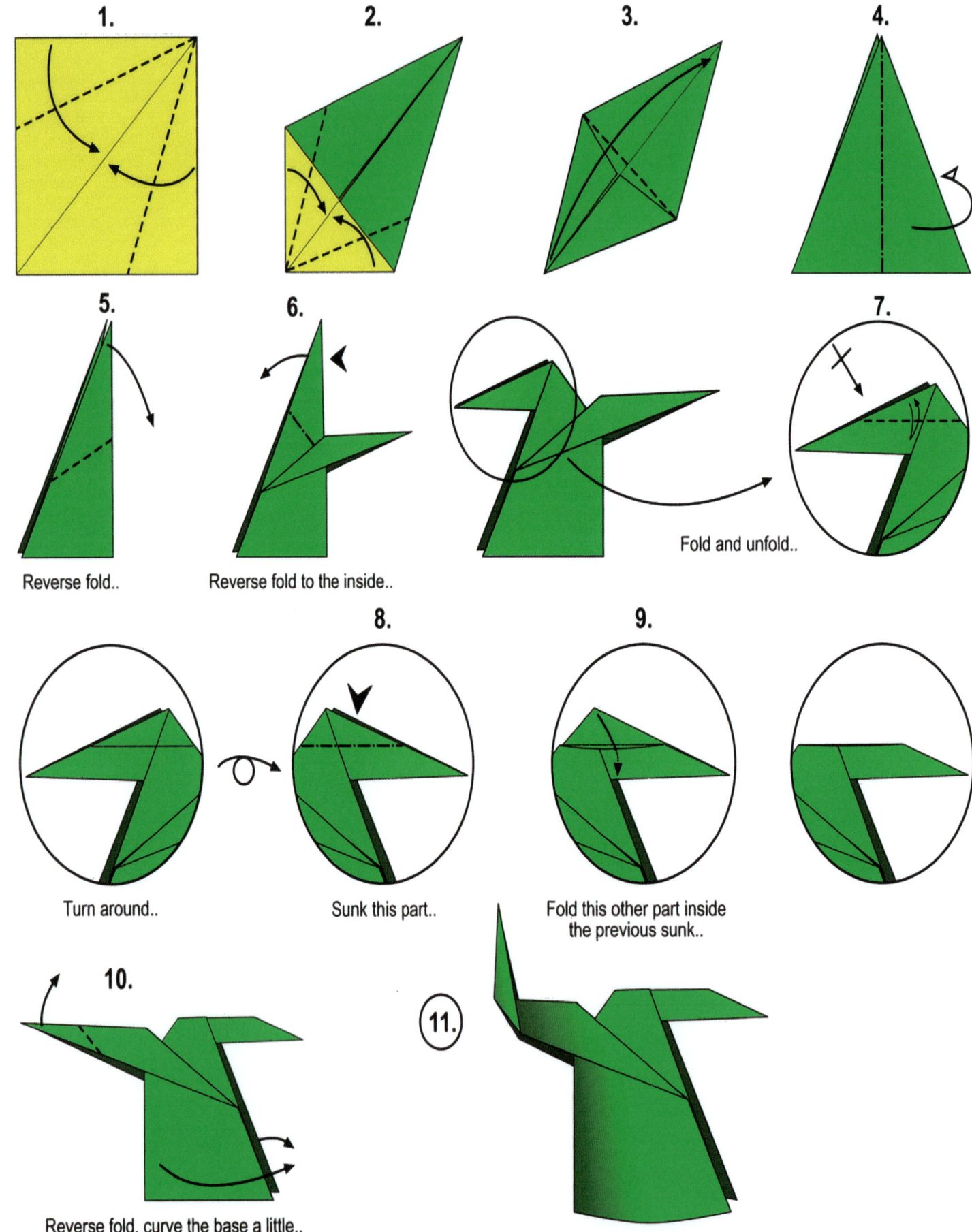

CRANE TSURU

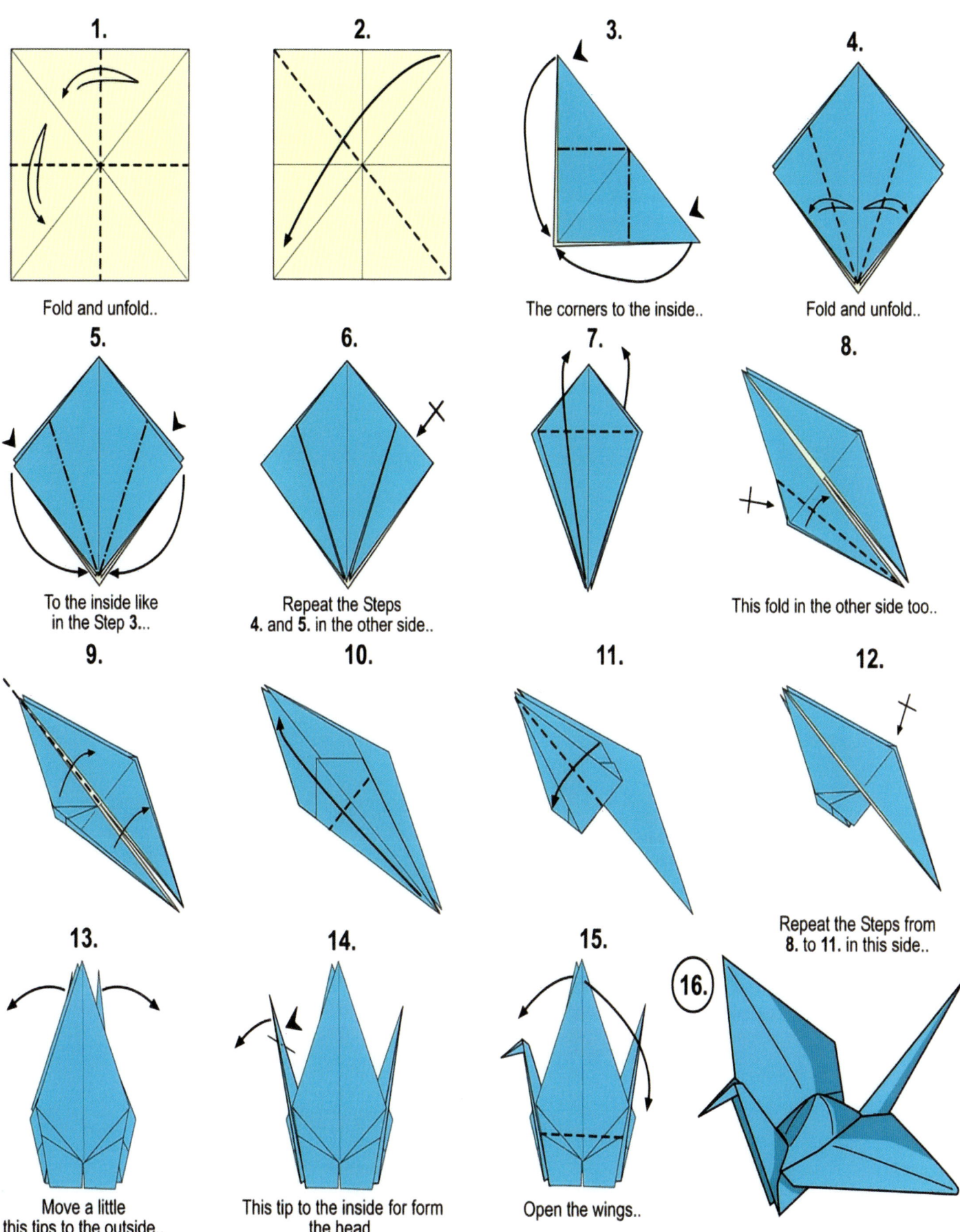

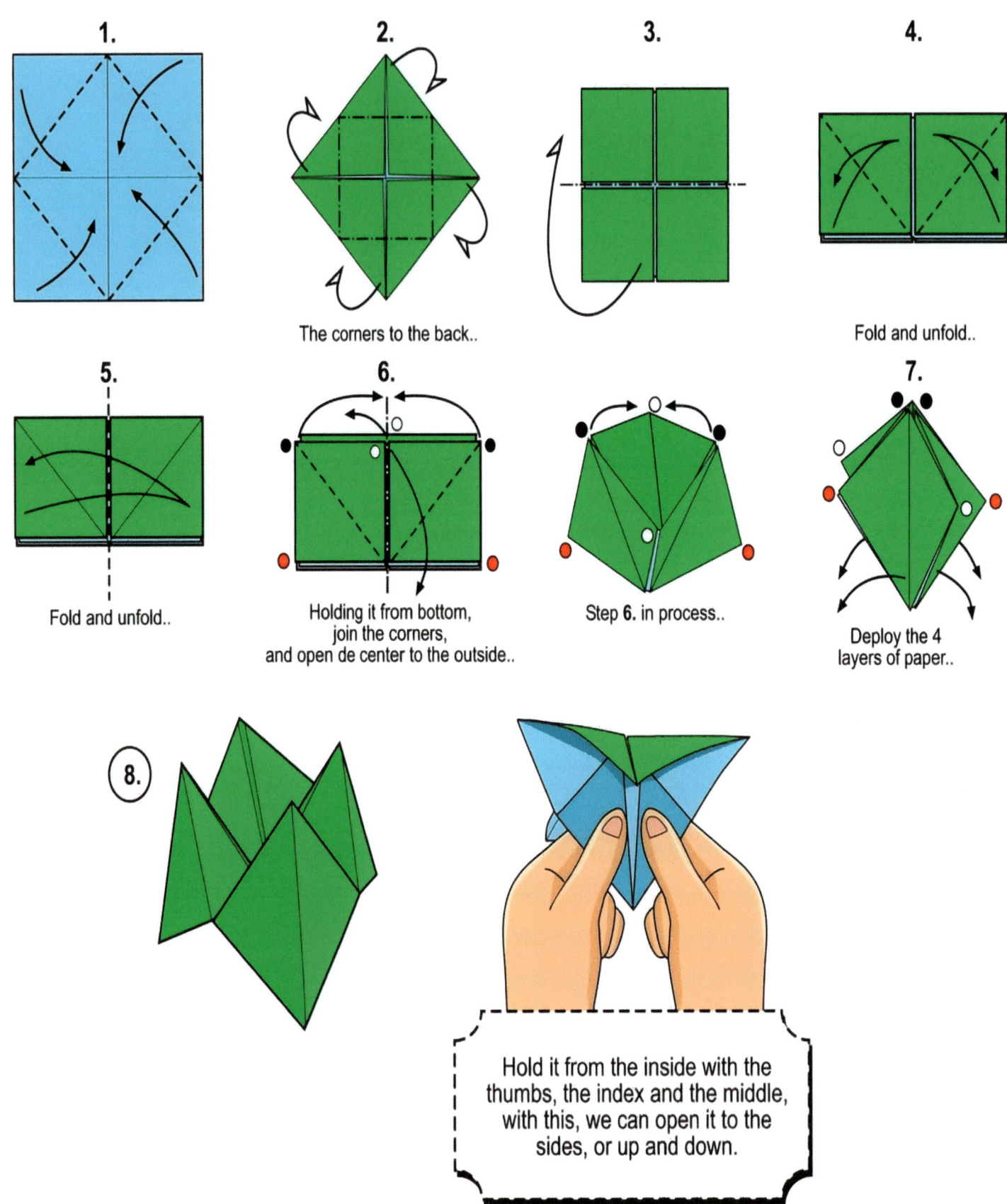

LOTUS

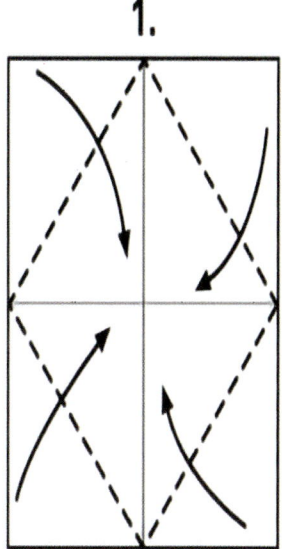
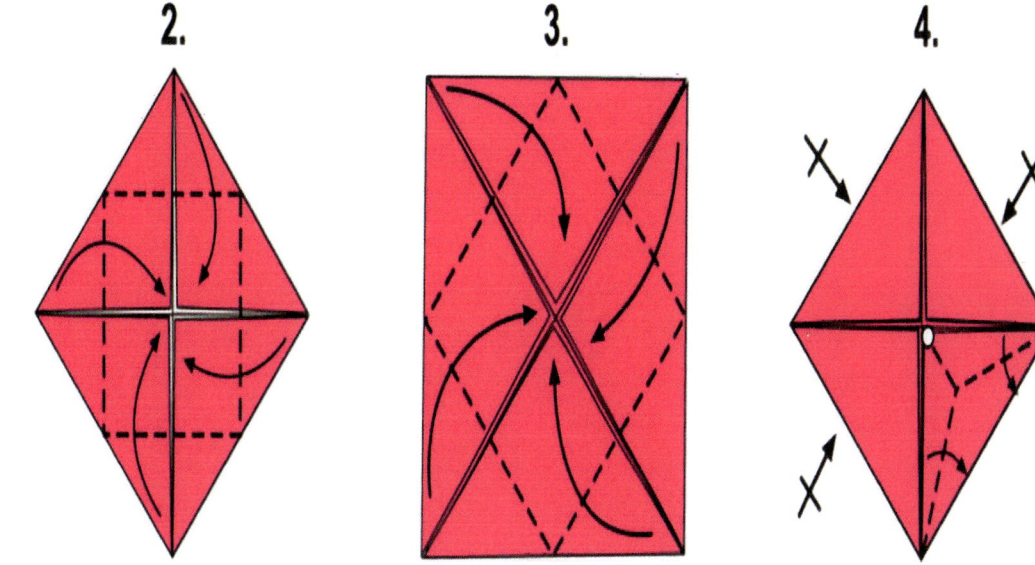

Fold the corners..

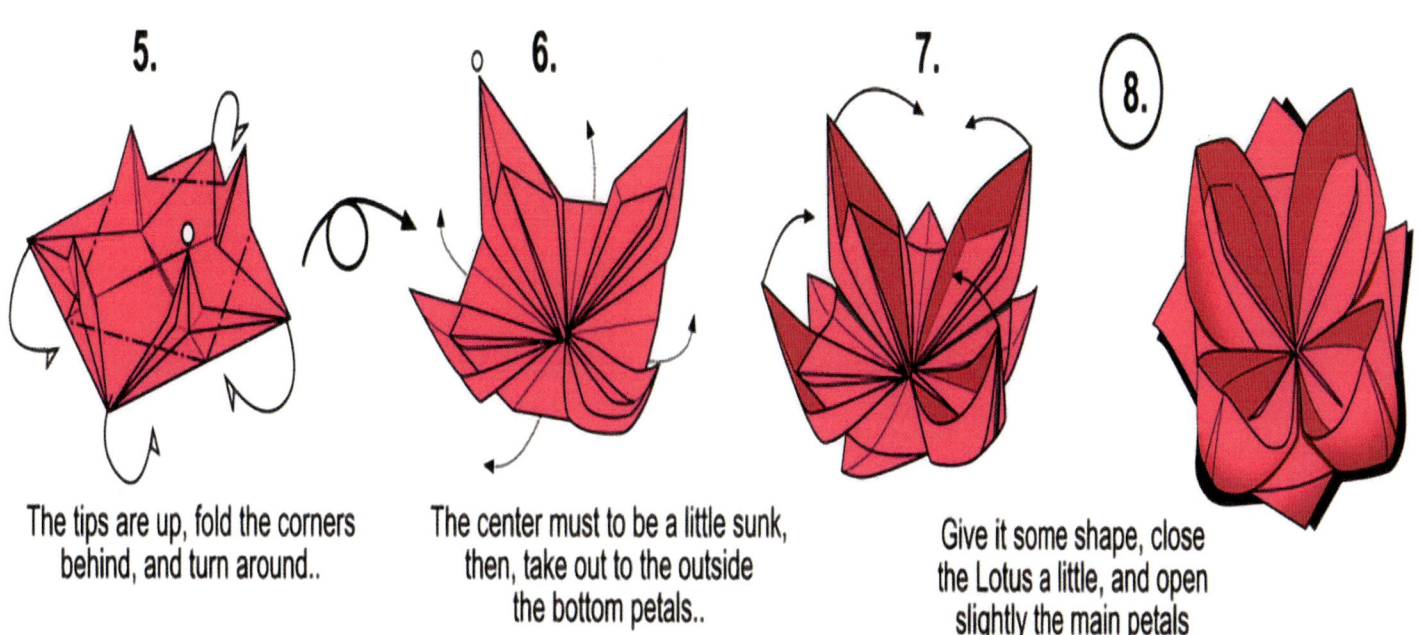

5. The tips are up, fold the corners behind, and turn around..

6. The center must to be a little sunk, then, take out to the outside the bottom petals..

7. Give it some shape, close the Lotus a little, and open slightly the main petals

HOUSE

1.
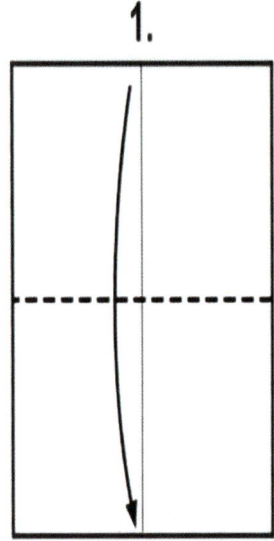

2.
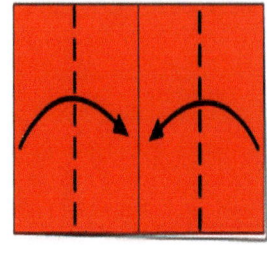
The sides to the center..

3.
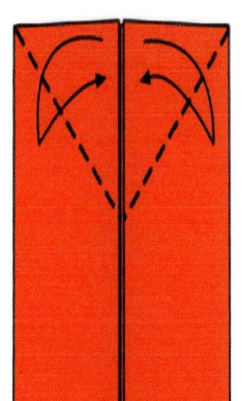
Fold and unfold..

4.
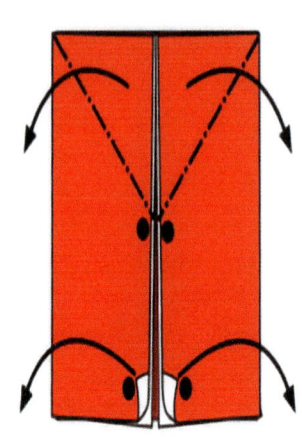
Open the top layers

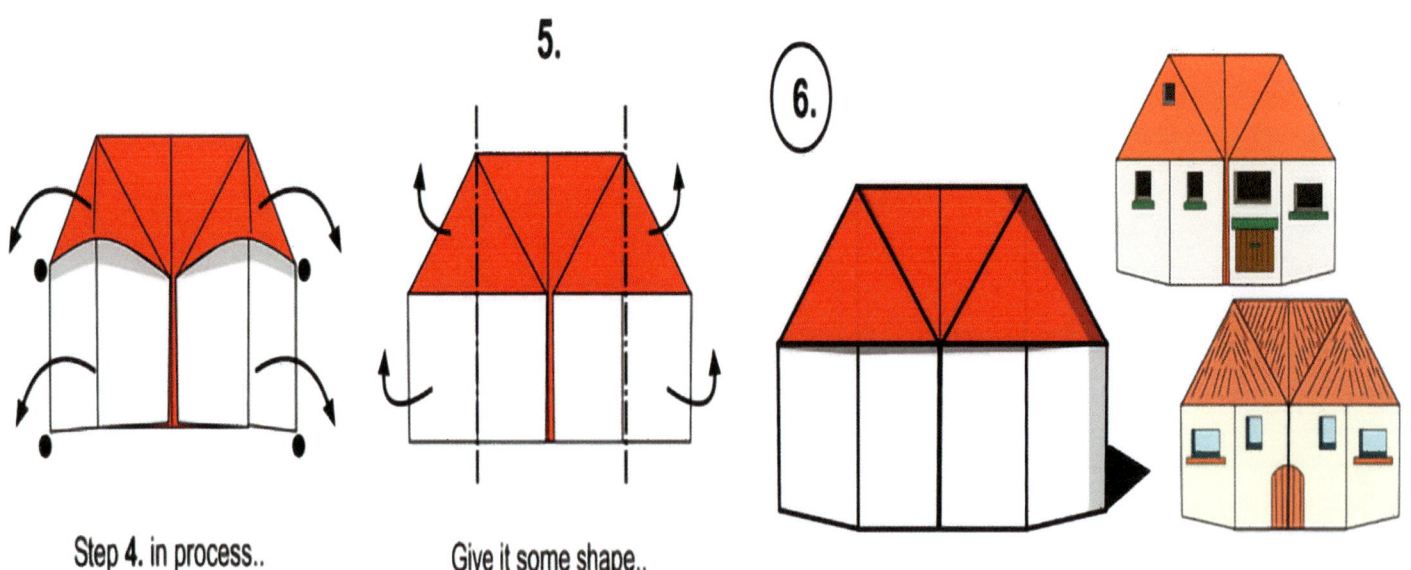

Step 4. in process..

5. Give it some shape..

6.

SHREW

1. Fold and unfold
2. Fold and unfold
3. Fold to the center
4.
5. Repeat the Steps 3. and 4. in this side
6. Open the layers to the sides and fold the tip down
7.
8.
9. Fold to the center
10.
11. Fold down and squash
12. Fold down and squash
13.
14. Sunk to the inside and fold down the leg
15. Repeat the Steps from 11. to 14. in this side
16. Fold and unfold
17.
18.
19.
20. Fold to the center
21.
22.
23.
24. Fold back, then to the front
25. 2 Reverse folds for the nose
26. Curve the tail and give some shape to the nose
27.

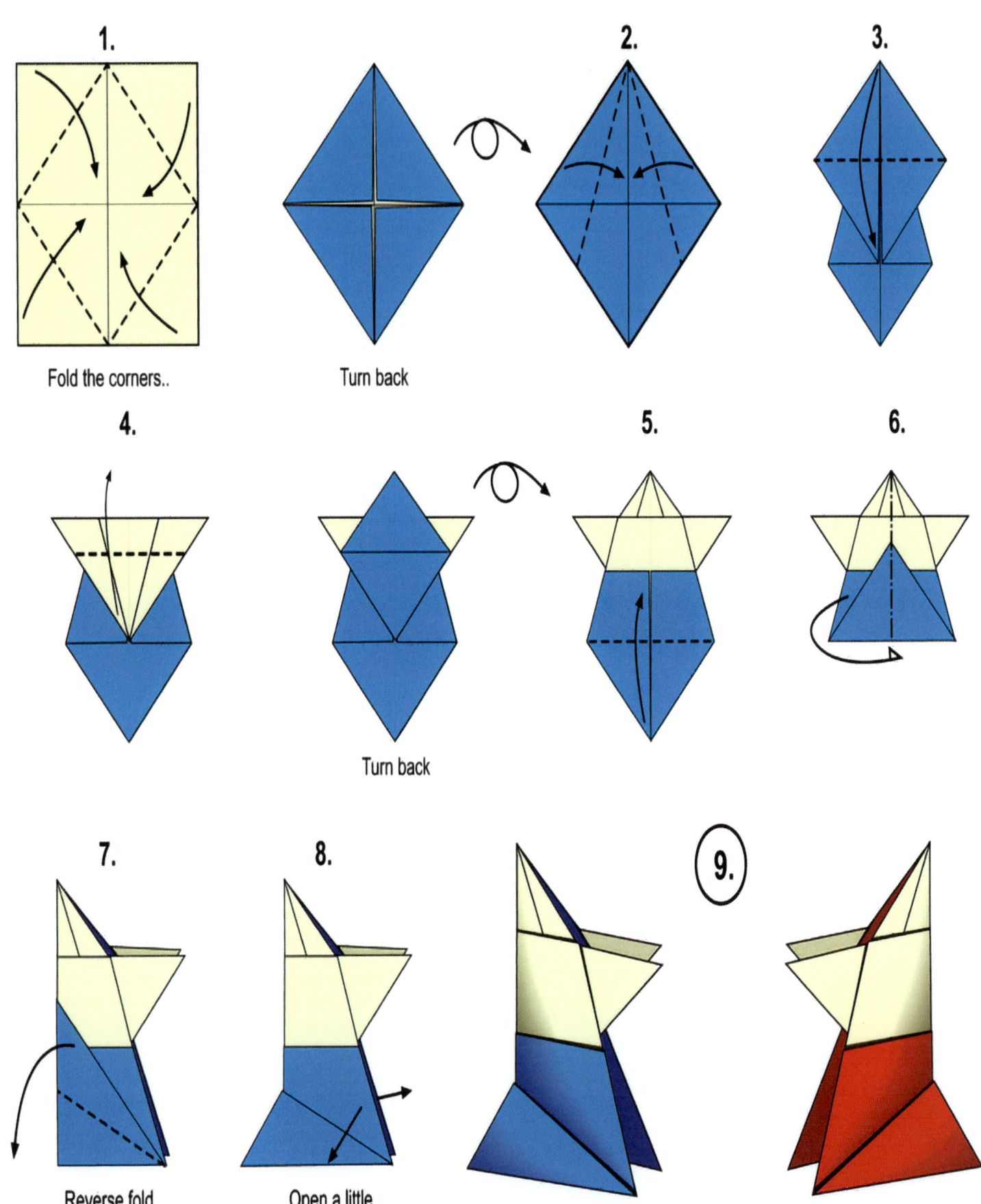

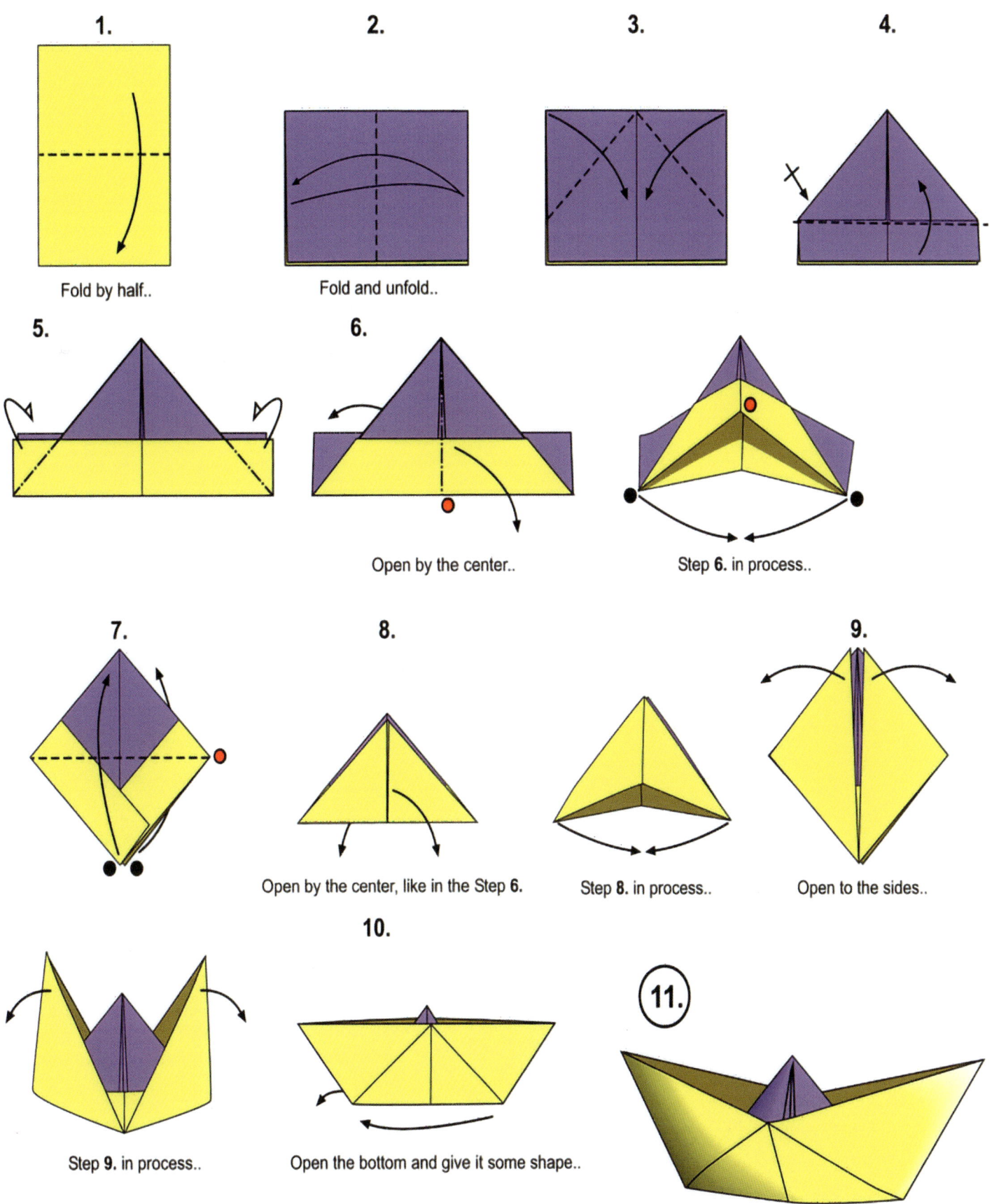

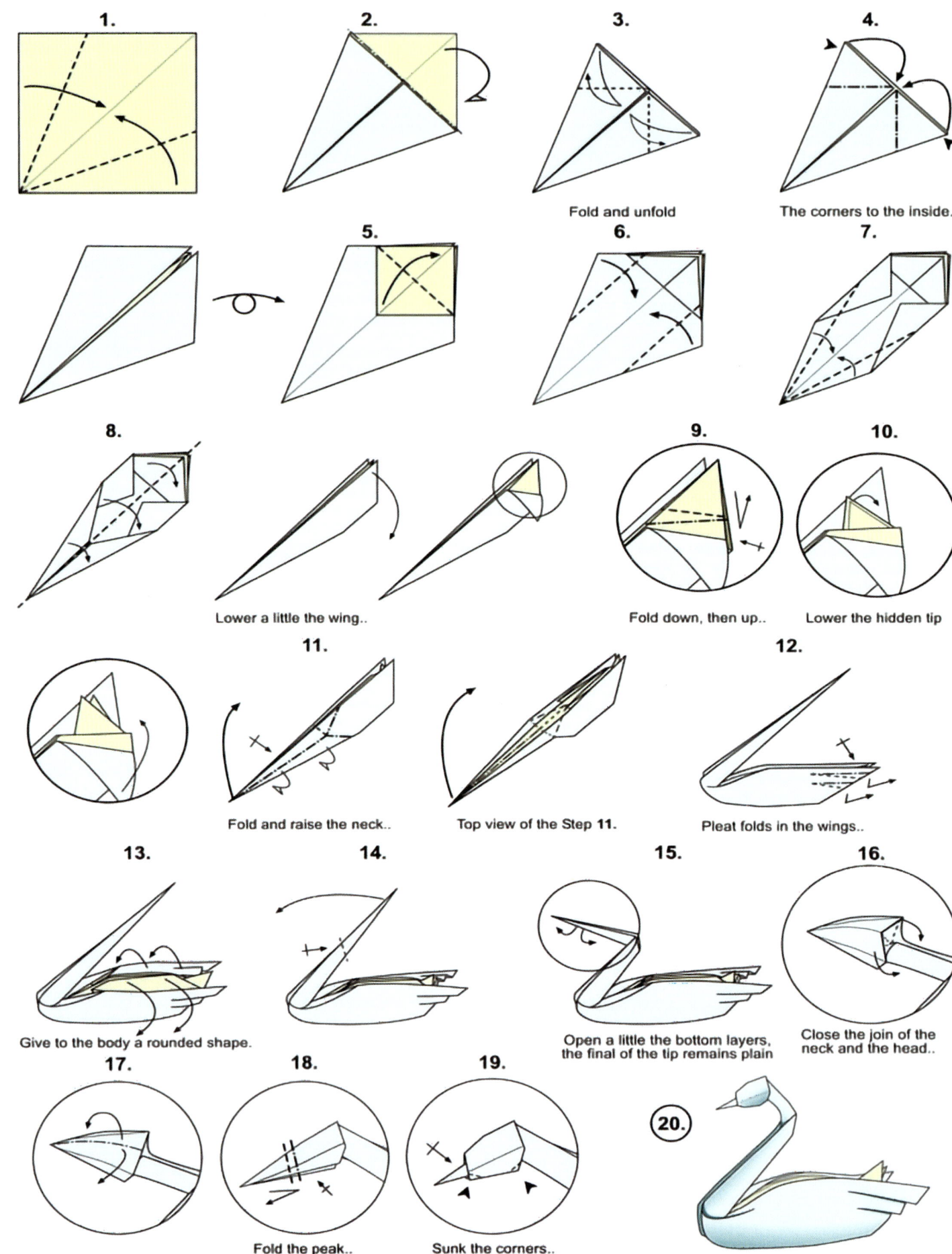

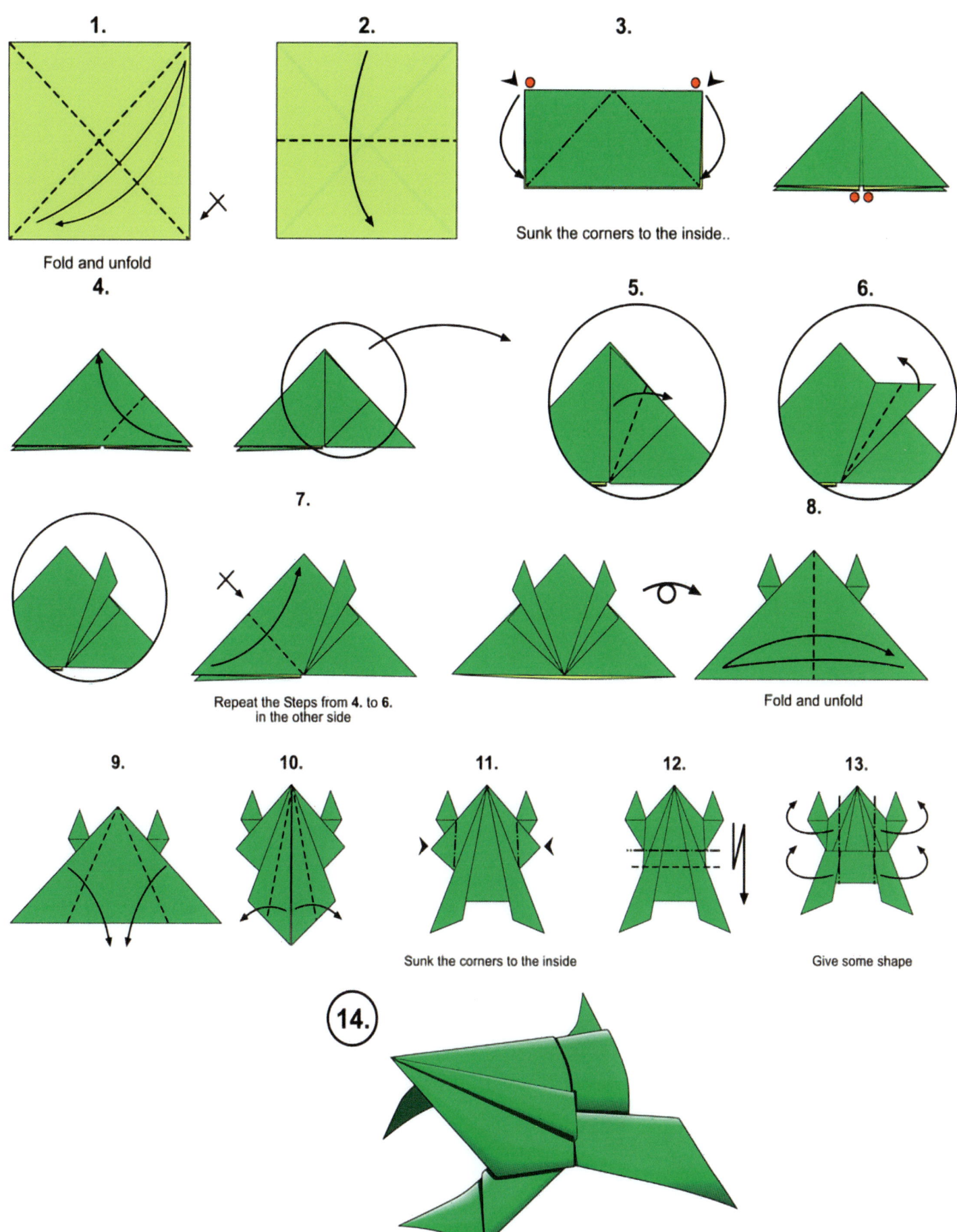

DART PLANE

1.

Fold the corners..

2.

3.

4.

5.

BASIC AERODYNAMIC

Flaps	Side stabilizers	Dihedral angle
Flaps up: The plane ascends Flaps down: The plane descends	Helps to control the direction, with this, the plane's tip doesn't go to the sides during the flight	In some models, the inclined wings give better stability than the parallel wings

Wings parallel to the ground

Wings in Y

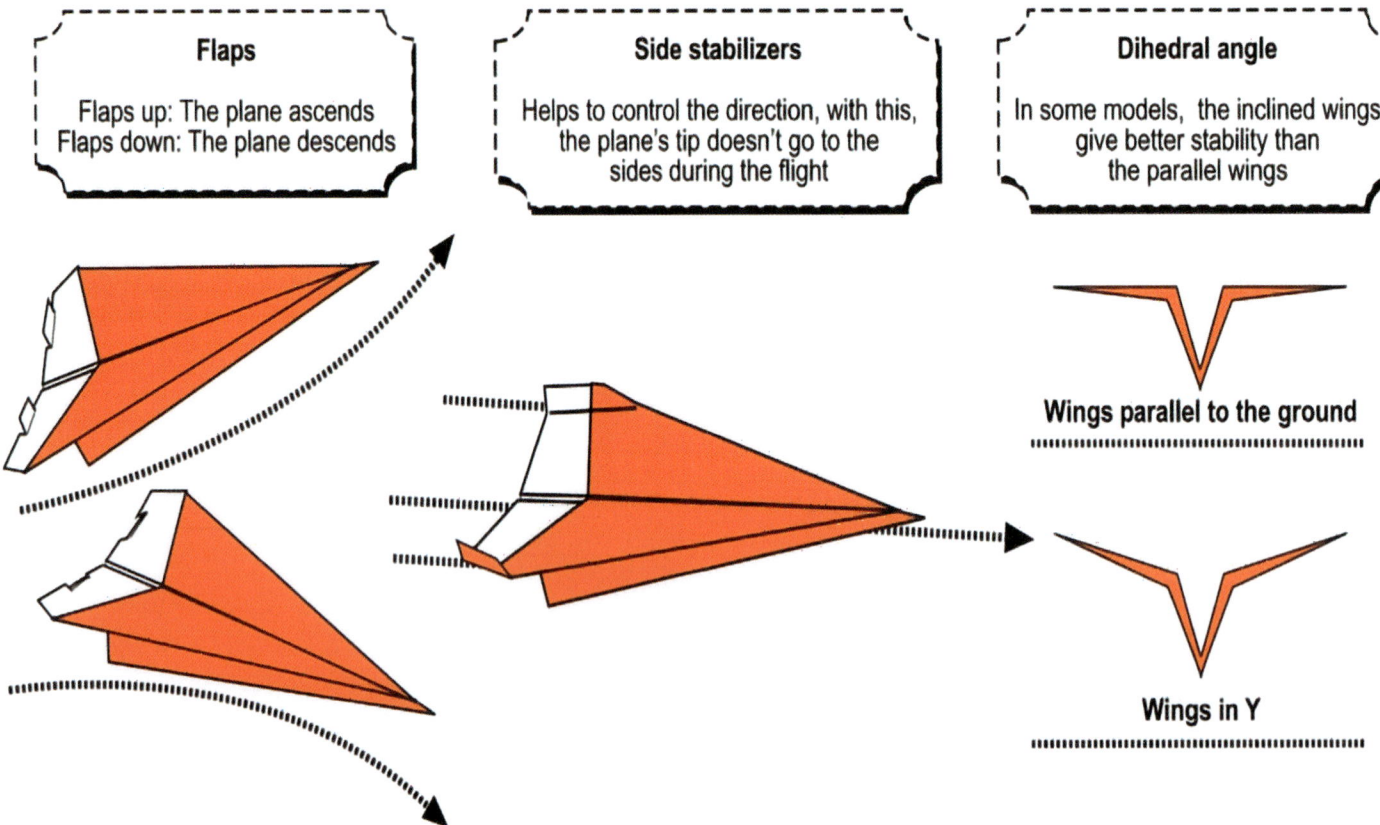

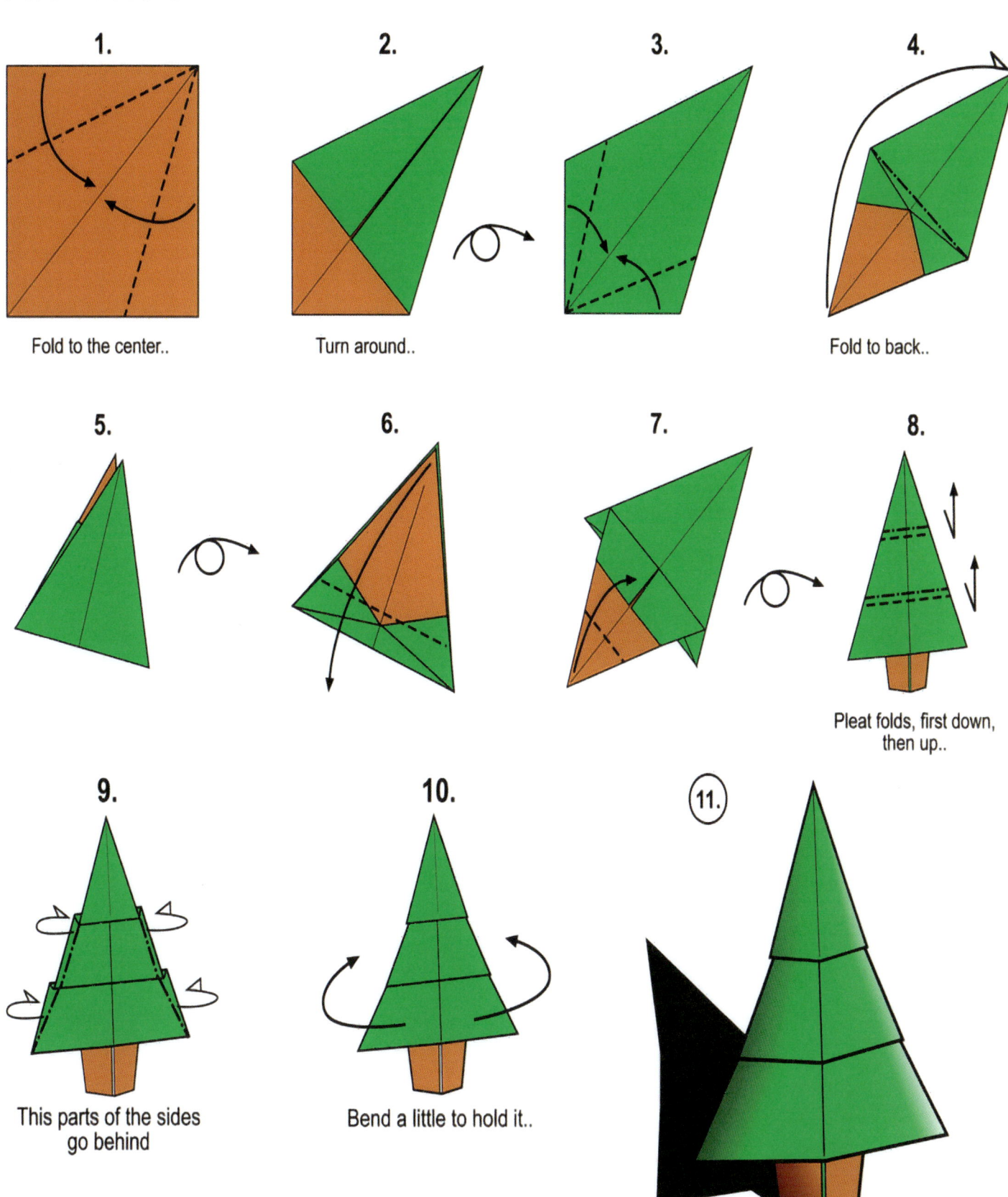

OWL

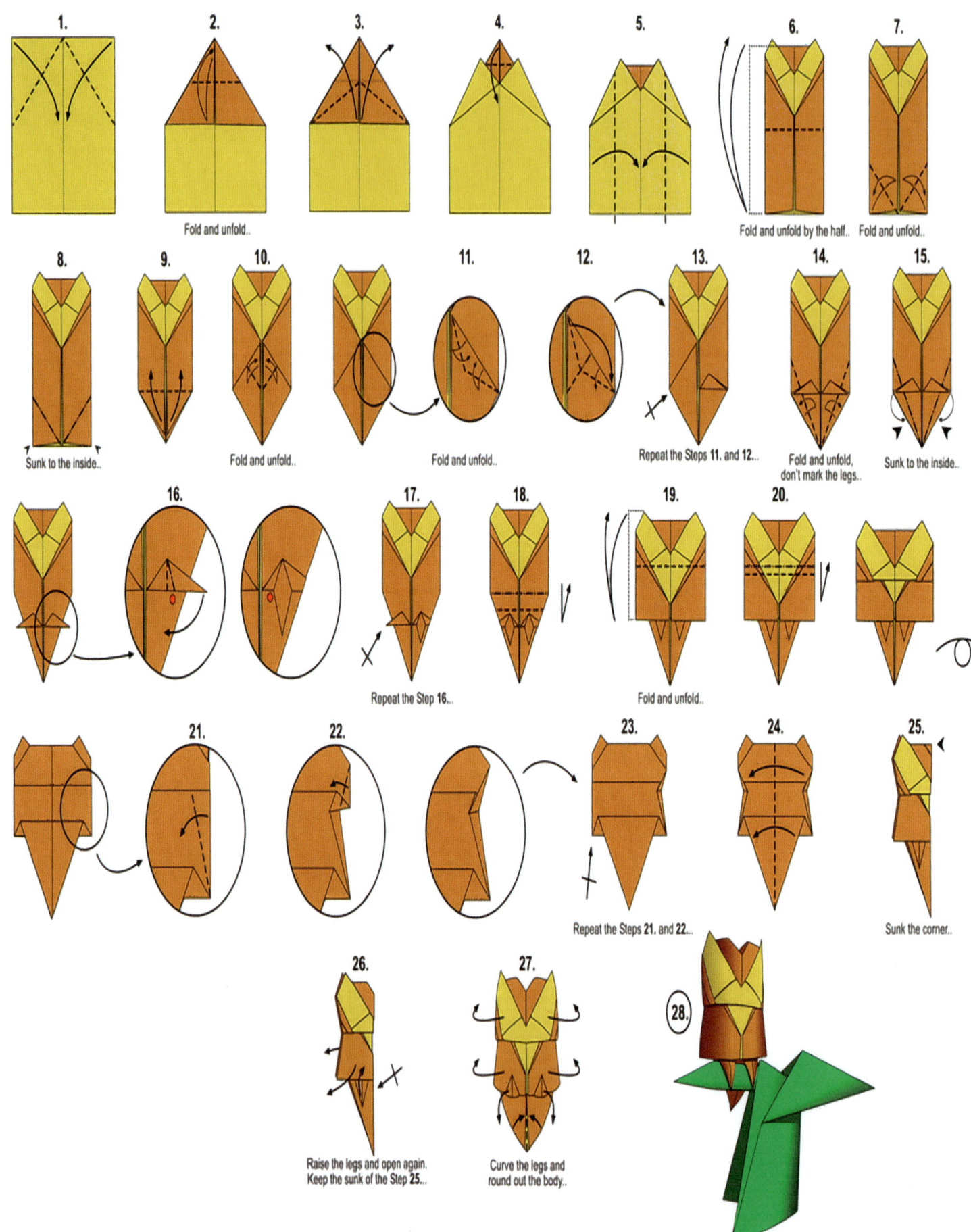

PLESIOSAURUS

1.
2.
3.
4.
5. Fold and unfold
6. Fold and unfold
7.
8.
9.
10.
11.
12.
13.
14.
15.
16. Repeat the Steps from 12. to 14. in this side
17. Sunk to the inside
18.
19. Sunk the neck part
20.
21.
22. Raise the neck, first fold down, then fold up..
23. Fold the head..
24.
25. Fold a little to the inside and give some shape to the body
26.

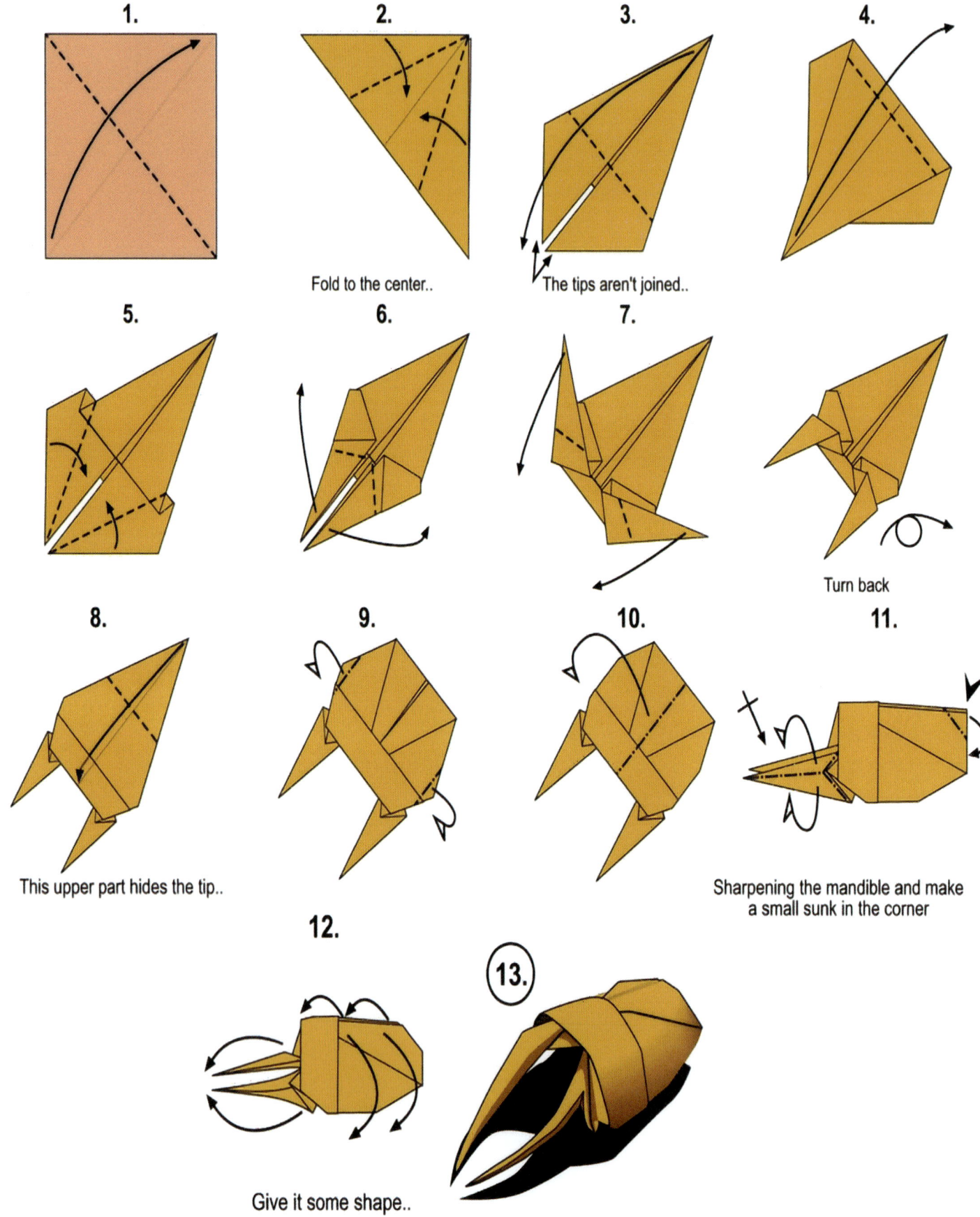

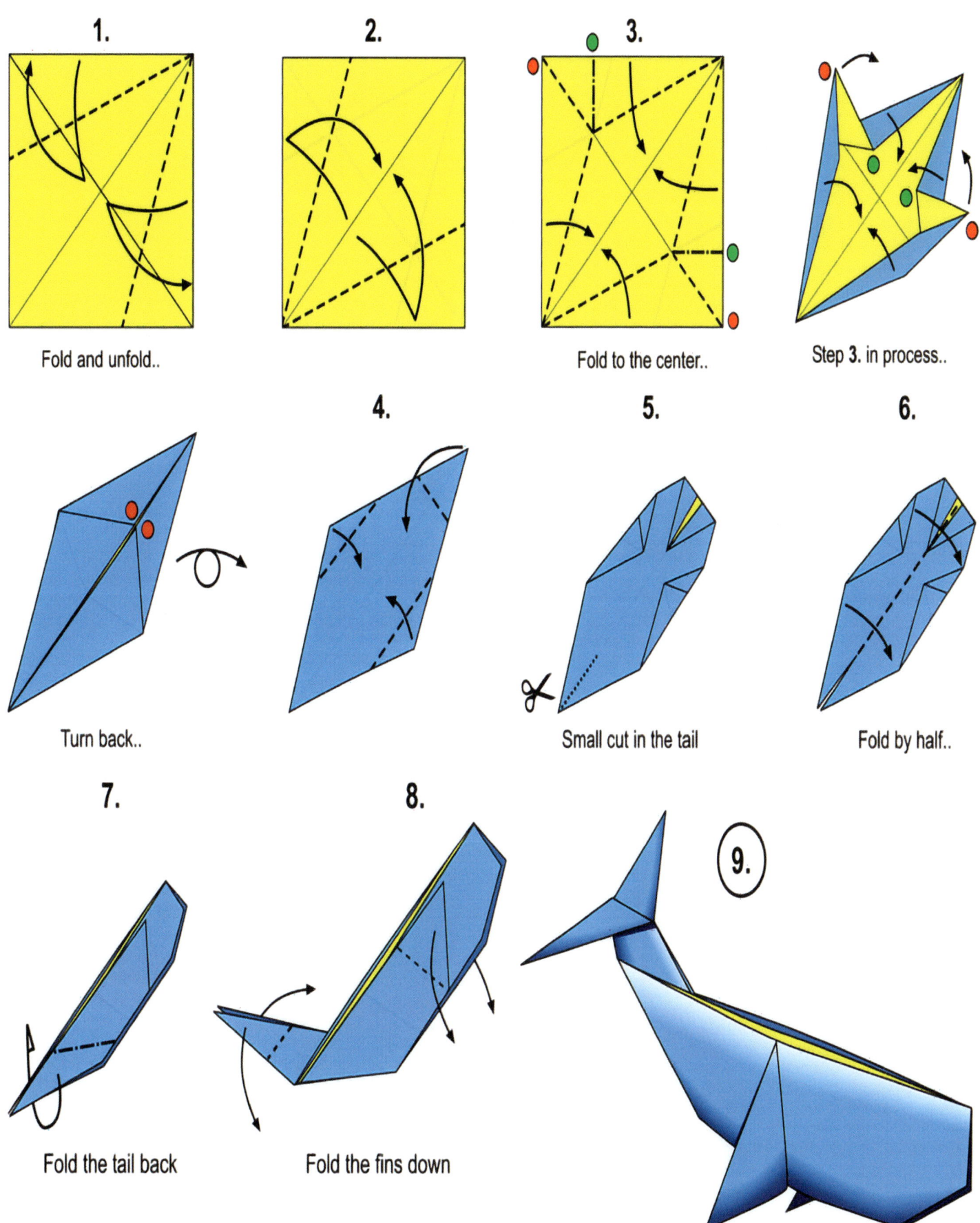

SAMPAN

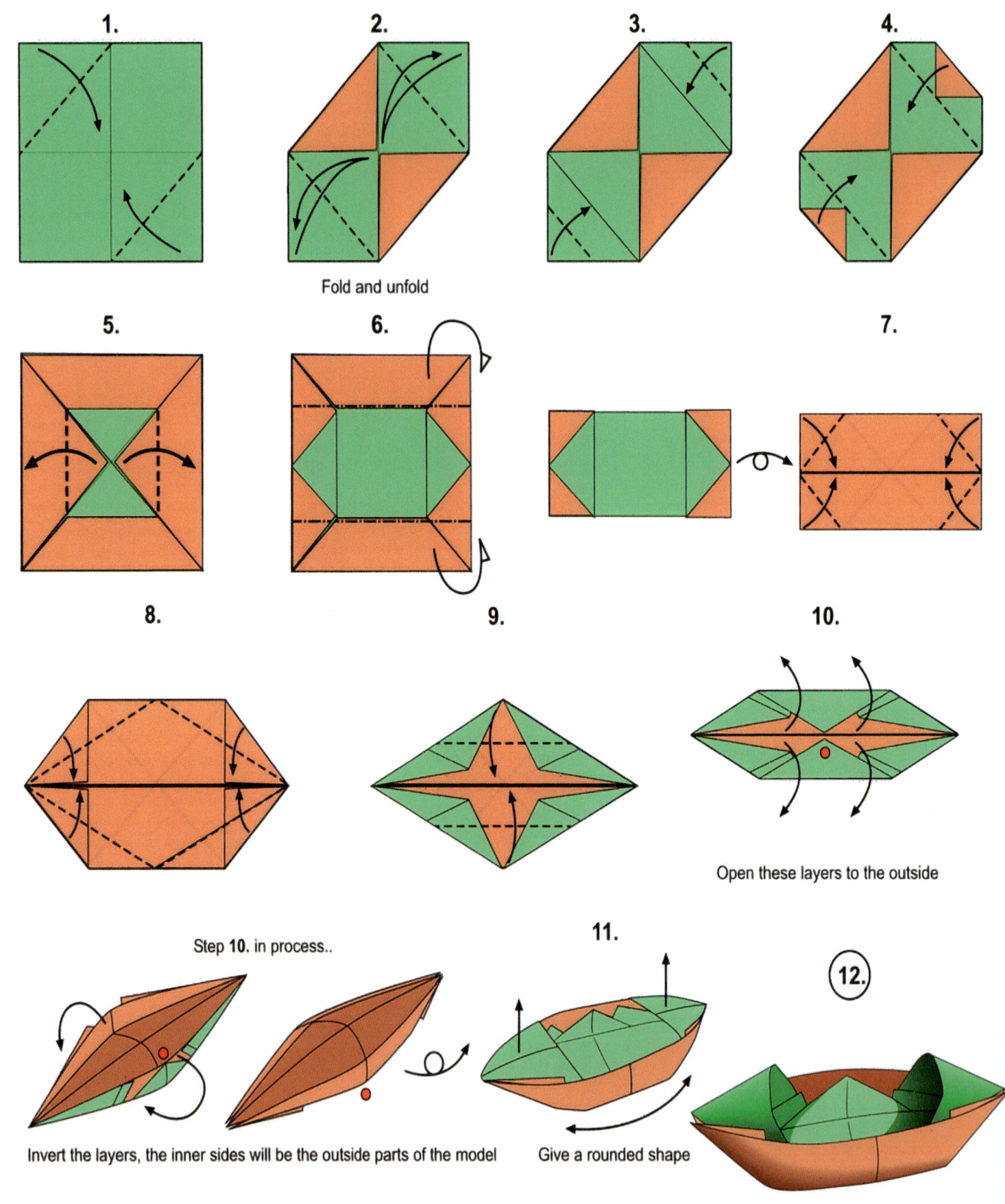

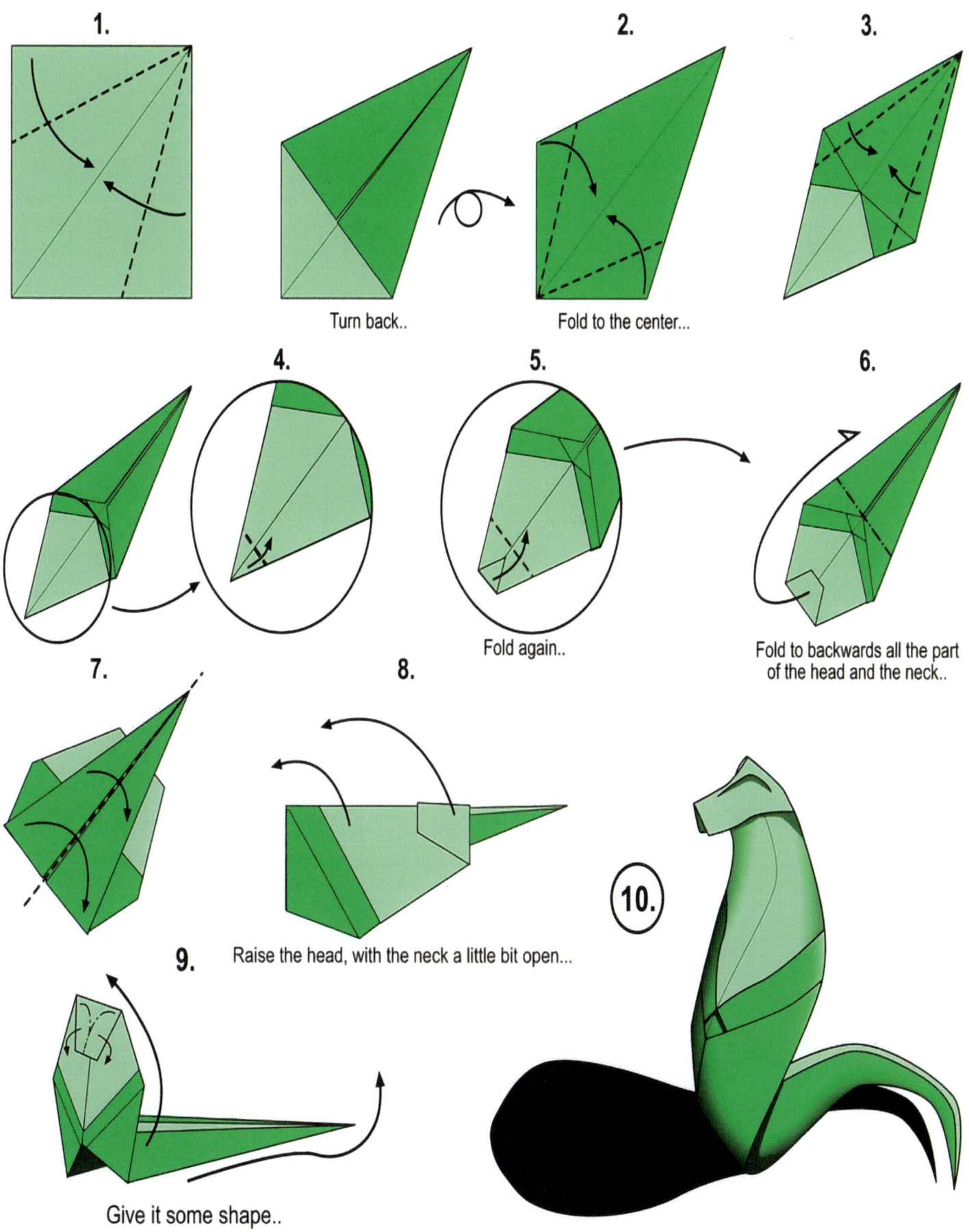

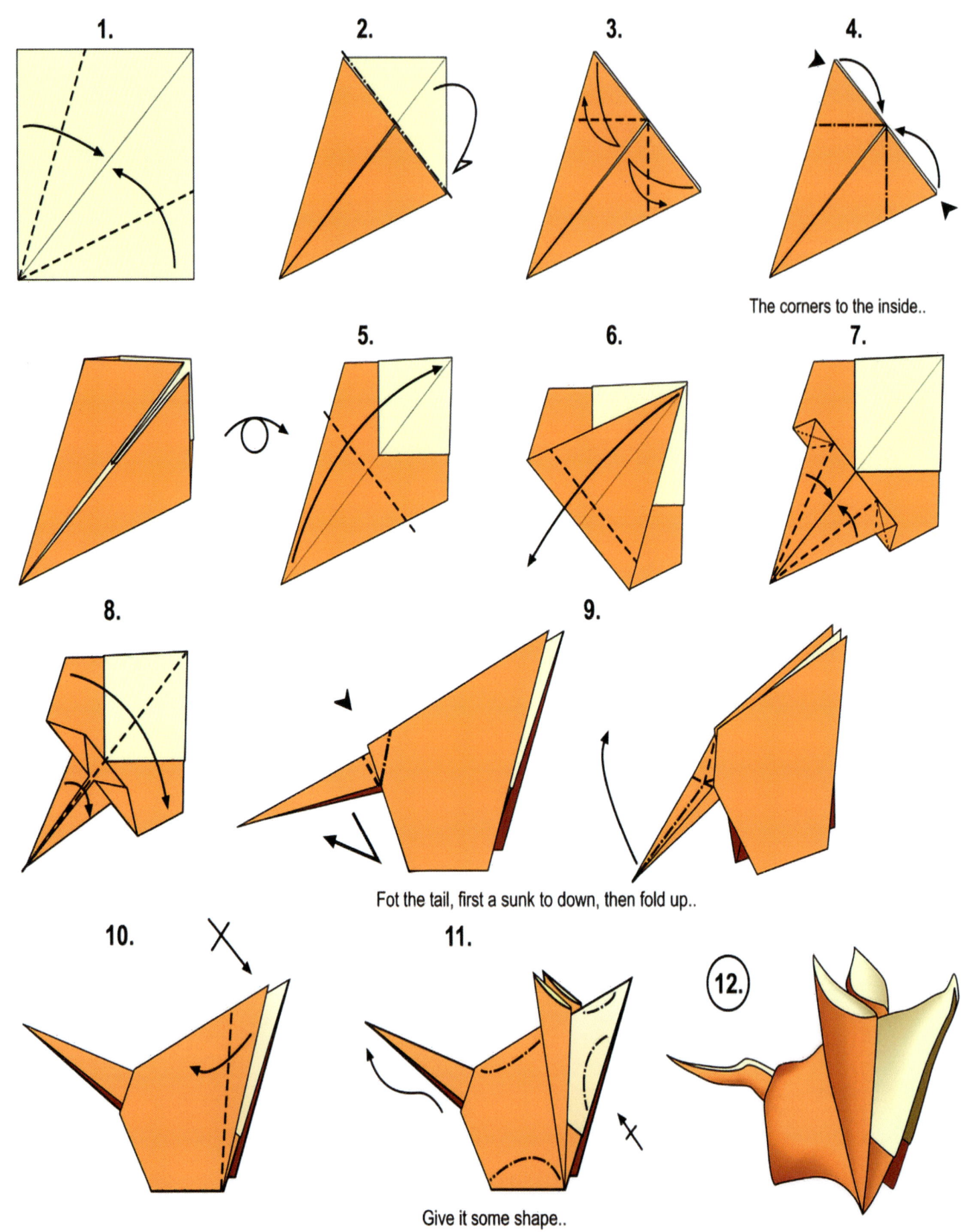

Printed in Great Britain
by Amazon